CONTENT CREATION
IN THE
DIGITAL AGE

STRATEGIES

TO STAND OUT

Churchill Stevenson

Copyright©2024 Churchill Stevenson

All Rights Reserved

INTRODUCTION

EASY STEPS TO CONTENT CREATION

1. Establish Your Goals:
2. Determine Who Your Audience Is:
3. Choose Your Format:
4. Generate and Brainstorm Ideas:
5. Research:
6. Outline Your Content:
7. Create Your Content:
8. Edit and Revise:
9. Optimize for SEO (Search Engine Optimization):
10. Publish and Promote:
11. Engage with Your Audience:
12. Evaluate Performance:

THE USE OF AI IN CONTENT CREATION

6 Ways for Creating Content with AI
AI Content Creation Tools

SOME PROFITABLE TOPICS ON CONTENT CREATION

CONTENT CREATION FORMATS
1. Blogs:
2. Podcast and Webinars
3. Videos:
4. Image-based Contents:

SOCIAL MEDIA POSTS

IDEAS FOR CREATING SOCIAL MEDIA CONTENT

COMMON MISTAKES CONTENT CREATORS MAKE AND HOW TO AVOID THEM

CONCLUSION

INTRODUCTION

So many people identify themselves today as "content creators". It is true that the creative economy is flourishing, offering the possibility of working from the comfort of your home while doing what you love most.

However, people believe that no training or experience is necessary. More so, your work does not necessarily need approval from anyone. This same allure of "anyone can make it" also makes the entry path into the field risky, as creators learn by trial and error. It is evident therefore, that creating professional content involves much more than meets the eye.

The process of coming up with ideas for blog posts, videos, infographics, and other content formats that appeal to your buyer persona, as well as crafting written or visual material around those ideas, is known as content creation. In other words, content creation involves the creation of content that resonates with your target audience and helps to support your business goals. Therefore, you're not just making content for your own sake here; rather, you're making it with particular personas, funnel stages, and KPIs in mind. The goal of all content is to establish a connection with your audience.

By producing informative, useful, and engaging content, you may win over your audience's trust and loyalty. And creating content that genuinely works to promote content marketing requires developing that trust.

The majority of beginners have the tendency to believe that creating content begins with you and what you wish to express. However, knowing your audience and visualizing what they value, find intriguing, and what prior content was attracted to them and why is actually the first step in the brainstorming process. It's important to create content that appeals to your audience rather than just talking about yourself. This entails being aware of what they are looking for in Google and other social media platforms.

Similar to your knowledge, your skills are a business. You may become an expert in something you're good at and make money doing it while you help others learn and apply what you know. Your days can be focused and organised around what you enjoy doing if you know how to use your knowledge and then, go on to work for yourself on your own schedule from home.

If you do not know how to do it correctly, creating content can be a laborious task. Thus, I am going to teach you in this guide how to produce powerful, captivating content that advances your company objectives without sacrificing your sanity in the process and make you to stand out.

EASY STEPS TO CONTENT CREATION

Creating great content starts with a well-established process. Generally speaking, information that is helpful is inherently, effectively and more captivating than content created just for the sake of creation. Pay attention to topics that your audience may use for their everyday lives. Be practical in your approach by finding answers to questions like: What issues are you trying to resolve with your content? What attracts people to your work? What value do you convey to or provide your audience? Concentrate on this aspect of problem-solving and imagine yourself in your audience's position rather than creating from your own viewpoint and continuously trying to come up with fresh, innovative ideas.

Discuss your professional or personal journey as a content creator rather than keeping your content generic. Which major achievements have you made? Better still, discuss your shortcomings. Tell us what you took away from your failures and how they affected your future approaches to situations. Talk about the highs and lows you've experienced; people are interested in hearing about both.

Whether you're producing films, images, articles, or any other type of content, creating content may be a rewarding experience. To assist you in getting started with content development, consider these simple steps:

1. Establish Your Goals: In an attempt to grab the attention of their audience and potential buyers, content creators fail to take the time upfront to define a clear purpose and a specific desired customer and or audience action for their blogs, podcasts, case studies, thought leadership or opinion pieces. There is an inherent danger in this approach. Adopting this mindset will probably result in a piece of content that is unfocused and untargeted, which will definitely fall short of your expectations. In the always changing world of social media, it is essential to have a well-considered plan and a well thought out goal in place before clicking the "post" button.

All too frequently, people upload their ideas, photos, and updates without stopping to ask themselves two basic questions: Why am I sharing this, and for whom am I posting it? Take a time to consider your goals before sharing anything on social media. Are you trying to sell a good or service, educate, entertain or inspire people? Your content should be driven by your goal.

Each and every content you create must have a purpose and should contribute to one or more overarching marketing objectives. You should be able to explain to anyone why you decided to write that blog post or create that infographic.

2. Determine Who Your Audience Is: Be aware of the audience for whom you are creating content. Knowing the tastes, needs, and interests of your audience will help you create content that appeals to them. As you progress in the process, you'll be able to come up with better, more powerful content ideas if you know what matters to your audience. To enable you effectively identify your audience, ask yourself questions like:

i. Who Makes Up My Audience? Fundamental questions or statistics on age, interests, education, location and purchasing habits will go a long way in identifying your audience, and you can expand from there. For example, if you know that your target audience is recent high school graduates, your content generation strategy will focus accordingly.

ii. What is My Audience Aware of Already? What Are They Ignorant of? This enables you to minimize reliability, provides a general overview, and reduces the risk of assumption of what your audience already understands. Again, fundamental questions can help: how well does my target audience know my company or product? What preconceptions or stereotypes do they hold? Perhaps you are speaking to an audience that is already partially expert, such as lawyers or bankers. Make sure your content is tailored to your audience's requirements, education, and reading level.

iii. What Matters to My Audience? What is it that do not Matter to Them? Make a list of your audience's top concerns and label them. In what way does this complement the services your company offers? These principles of alignment serve as building blocks for producing informative content that engenders audience loyalty and trust. For instance, it could be a major selling factor for certain audience members if all of your products and or services are AI driven.

3. Choose Your Format: The various media available for presenting your online content include blog entries, podcasts, films, infographics, ebooks, and lots more. Selecting the appropriate format for your content based on your audience, objectives, and available resources can significantly impact its effectiveness.

The question however, is how can you choose the best format for every piece of content? Here are some pointers to assist you in selecting the ideal content format for creating material on the internet.

Choose the kind of material you wish to produce. Posts on social media, podcasts, videos, infographics, and blogs are among the options. Select a format that fits both your audience's preferences and your skill level. Understanding your audience and their preferences is the first step towards selecting a content type. When it comes to viewing online material, different audiences could have varied expectations, habits, and interests. For instance, certain audiences could find it more enjoyable to watch a video than to read a lengthy piece, while others would like to listen to a podcast while exercising or during their commute. You can find out more about the demographics, interests, problems, and content consumption habits of your audience by utilizing technologies like social media, analytics, and surveys. Knowing your audience allows you to personalize your content format to their specific demands and preferences. Varied content formats may have varied strengths and limitations in terms of message delivery, audience engagement, and desired actions. For instance, blog postings may be fantastic for SEO, education, and lead generation, whereas videos may be wonderful for brand awareness, entertainment, and social sharing.

Considering your objectives and available resources, you can set specific, measurable, achievable, relevant, and time-bound (SMART framework) goals for your content. Defining your goals allows you to align your content format with your targeted outcomes. Different material formats may necessitate varying amounts of time, money, expertise, and technologies to produce and disseminate. Making a high-quality video, for instance, can take more resources than writing a blog post, and making an infographic might call for more design expertise than writing an ebook. When it comes to producing and disseminating various information types, you can assess your strengths, weaknesses, opportunities, and threats using a SWOT analysis. You can select a content format that works with your resources, capabilities, and timetable by evaluating your options.

Taking inspiration from other online content creators in your industry or area of interest is one of the best ways to determine what format to use for your content. You can find instances of content creators who are successful and use a variety of content types, then examine what works for them. Additionally, you can search for holes or openings where your content format can provide something special or novel. In order to identify and track popular and trending content formats in your business or specialty, you can make use of social media and Google Trends. You can gain ideas and knowledge for your own content format decisions by studying from others.

4. Generate and Brainstorm Ideas: Make a list of the subjects or ideas you wish to address in the content of your piece. Think on what your audience would find important or fascinating, as well as what fits with your area of expertise or interest. Ask questions if you are in doubt. The following approach will be of help:

i. Ask the Audience: This doesn't have to be a clear-cut "help me" request or anything similarly apparent; instead, it might be subtle and seamless. Examine your audience's preferences for your content and discover any areas where they may not be as engaged. To better target your future approach, do a straw poll or go into the details with your audience. You might be surprised to learn that what you believe to be effective could not be what your audience finds most endearing or even what they remember you for.

ii. Ask a Friend: If you're at a loss for inspiration, speak with a confidante or friend. Use a friend, relative or coworker to offer input or to assist generate ideas if you feel uncomfortable asking the audience.

iii. Ask the Expert: Identify and profile a more experienced person. Explore a topic that interests your audience but about which you know nothing. It's likely that your audience will value the possibility to advance their skills as a result of your learning. This is another efficient use of your time; all you have to do is pose a few questions or look into a specific topic or niche, and your subject will be able to elaborate, clarify, and instruct. In the end, the content produces itself.

iv. Ask a Guest: Use guest posts as a way to give someone else in your field visibility through your platform. A guest post or full takeover will vary your material, provide your audience with an alternative voice or viewpoint, and temporarily shift attention from you so you can concentrate on brainstorming new ideas.

5. Research: Collect facts, figures, and resources pertaining to the subject you have selected. This will enable you to offer your audience valuable content that is factual and informative. You can do this effectively using:

i. Internet: Almost everyone with something valuable these days has it uploaded to the internet. You may find information on almost anything on the internet, including products and services, general interest, sports, health, the environment, science, and technology, among other topics. Thus, search the internet for the data you require regarding your topic.

ii. Library: Everything that you require for a successful future has already been written. Almost everything you want to do right now has already been done and put in black and white by someone else, (i.e. write it down in a book, magazine or journal e.t.c.). It just requires you to visit the library to get such information for your content.

iii. Personal Journal: Personal journals are just notepads or jotters where you can scribble down thoughts. Gather good ideas, but don't rely on your memory. Your personal notebook is the greatest location to gather all the ideas and facts that come your way. Never think of your brain as a filing cabinet. Utilize your brain to solve difficulties and come up with solutions; record insightful thoughts in a notebook.

6. Outline Your Content: Make a basic structure or plan for your content. Make a logical arrangement of your thoughts and choose the primary topics you wish to discuss. You must create an outline of what material comes first and so on in order to keep your thoughts organized and your information flowing naturally. Your audience will be able to comprehend and value your report more readily as a result.

7. Create Your Content: Based on your outline, begin creating your content through writing, filming, designing, or recording. Make an effort to communicate your point succinctly and effectively. To create quality contents, take the following into consideration:

i. Writing Place and Time: Selecting a certain time and location to compose your customized reports is advised. Everybody has a time of the day when they are most focused and able to think more clearly. Additionally, there are locations where we feel more organized and at ease when writing. It could be in our study or bedroom in the wee hours of the morning.

ii. Read More: You will have access to more information the more you read. As you learn new concepts that broaden your understanding, you will also gain a deeper understanding of your subject.

iii. Write More: Always learn to write. You will improve as a writer the more you write; be tenacious and try again if you don't succeed the first time.

8. Edit and Revise: Check your pieces for mistakes and for cohesion and clarity. Make the required changes to raise the caliber of the content you create. It is a good idea to edit your content about five times. In the first edit, check your spelling; in the second, check your grammar. Say it how you want it said in the third edit, and in the fourth, consider whether your content makes sense. Finally, go over the whole content.

9. Optimize for SEO (Search Engine Optimization): To increase your content's visibility and reach, optimize it for search engines. To make your material easier to find, use meta descriptions, relevant keywords, and other SEO strategies.

10. Publish and Promote: When you are done with your content, post it in the relevant channels or platforms. To reach your audience, share it via email newsletters, social media, and other pertinent means.

11. Engage with Your Audience: Keep an eye on interactions, comments, and feedback regarding the content you created. To create a community around the content you produce, reply to comments, address inquiries, and interact with your audience.

12. Evaluate Performance: With analytics tools, monitor how well your content is performing. Keep an eye on metrics like views, engagement, shares, and conversions to find out what's successful and where you can make improvements.

You can make your content creation process more efficient and effective, thereby, creating valuable, engaging content that resonates with your audience, by following the above steps.

The Use of AI in Content Creation

The process of creating and optimizing content using artificial intelligence technology is known as AI content production. This includes coming up with concepts, crafting copy, editing, and determining how engaged an audience is.

The days of using just a pen and paper to draft thoughts into reality are long gone. The potent AI-driven tools that today's content producers use can help ignite a spark that grows into a conflagration of interesting blog entries, videos, and social media posts.

Not only is artificial intelligence altering the game, but it is also establishing a whole new arena. It has the ability to help content producers throughout the whole creative process.

6 Ways for Creating Content with AI

1. Organize Thoughts or Brainstorm and Draft Outlines: You can instantly come up with hundreds of content ideas with AI content production tools. This translates to spending more time honing ideas rather than creating them from scratch.

Sophisticated AI content creation platforms go beyond simple brainstorming and may produce an elaborate outline that covers your subject matter thoroughly and makes sure the information flows naturally.

AI may assist you in coming up with fresh and original ideas for your content by identifying important topics to write about and assessing the interests of your audience. This can be especially helpful if you're under pressure to meet a deadline or are having trouble coming up with ideas.

2. Research Keywords and Cluster Subjects: Keyword research is an important element of content marketing, but it can be time-consuming and laborious to accomplish manually. Fortunately, AI tools are transforming the process by automating keyword development and grouping.

Begin by brainstorming phrases related to your expertise or topic. This initial list serves as the foundation for your keyword research tool, which can create hundreds of relevant keywords in seconds.

Beyond only generating keywords, artificial intelligence (AI) algorithms go a step further by organizing them into relevant topic clusters, which serve as the foundation of your SEO approach. This is especially useful because it helps you to develop more focused and targeted material on specific themes or concepts in your niche or area of interest.

3. Speed up Content Research: AI tools not only write the material but also make research easier, which is important for creating intelligent long-form content.

In the quick-paced world of digital marketing, every second matters. Being a solopreneur means that you frequently have to handle a lot of tasks and many hats at once. Content research is one area where AI may drastically reduce your workload.

What would take hours or days for human researchers to complete may be accomplished in seconds by machine learning algorithms, which can quickly scan through massive amounts of web data and extract insightful information about your topic.

4. Proofread and Edit your Drafts: Just imagine halving the duration of your content review process.

That is possible with the correct artificial intelligence (AI) tools, which will revolutionize the way we hone and polish our marketing messaging.

AI is like having a dedicated team member who is constantly willing to help polish every line for impact; it does more than just provide edit suggestions.
Super intelligent generative AI chatbots may alter your content in real time.

5. Test for Plagiarism: Plagiarism is the intentional or inadvertent taking of credit for another person's words or ideas without properly citing the source.

Content is generated by generative AI techniques using the original datasets that they have been trained on. Because of this, some of its output can seem strikingly similar to already-published web content, which would be considered plagiarism.

However, it is good to know that we can now assess whether our AI-generated material sounds too robotic or plagiarizes other websites thanks to technology that powers AI. This is possible because a given artificial intelligence tool is check marked by another type of artificial intelligence tool.

6. Optimize Your Social Media Presence: In the busy world of social media, it can be difficult to stand out. But what would happen if you possessed a secret weapon?

AI technologies give your posts an extra boost, acting as your behind-the-scenes crew.

AI recommends hashtags that fit the tone of your brand. Consider it your friend with the perfect words to whisper in the social algorithms' ears.

To lure viewers in, captions ought to be engaging or thought-provoking. Imagine an AI content creation tool creating those ideal sentences for you; it would be like having a creative genius at your disposal.

Even when using social media, we consume with our eyes first. AI image generators can help with that by presenting eye-catching images that grab attention.

It is a fact that a picture can say a thousand words; when, however, a sophisticated writing assistance writes a captivating caption for it, the result could be compelling.

As you are aware, hashtags are essential to discoverability games. AI technologies can take on the labor-intensive task of creating pertinent tags, relieving you of the burden.

It will not be necessary to speculate as to which

hashtag might work best for your article or trend. Machine learning solutions provide options that are specifically catered to your audience based on their knowledge.

AI Content Creation Tools
Artificial intelligence (AI) content creation tools use technology to create text-based or visual material in response to written cues.

There are a wide range of AI content creation tools that are frequently used by content creators. These include OwlyWriter AI, ChatGPT, Midjourney, JasperAI, Canva, Murf and Synthesia and lots more. Just surf the internet to know the ones that suit your content type. While some are good for graphics and videos, others are for podcast while still others are for writing. You can get reviews to let you know which one is good for you.

Sustaining long-term growth through long-form content marketing requires striking a balance between AI efficiency and human creativity. AI tools can be used to generate ideas or expedite the process, but in order to make the content genuinely yours, you must always add your own voice and touch.

SOME PROFITABLE TOPICS ON CONTENT CREATION

Trends, audience interest, and demand from customers are some of the variables that influence profitable content creation topics. The following are some timeless and popular topics that have shown to be lucrative for content producers:

1. Personal Finance and Investing: Retirement planning, stock investment, real estate, budgeting, and saving money are evergreen and popular topics that are very lucrative.

2. Productivity and Personal Growth: Contents that offer guidance on enhancing personal and professional lives, such as goal-setting, habit building and time management, are in great demand.

3. Technology and Gadgets: Tech-savvy audiences are drawn to reviews, tutorials, and updates on the newest devices, software, and trends in technology.

4. Well-being, Fitness and Health: There is always a need for content on self-care, mental health, exercise, and nutrition, especially with the growing emphasis on wellbeing.

5. Beauty and Fashion: Audiences who are serious about grooming and personal style are drawn to product reviews, styling advice, makeup tutorials, and fashion trends.

6. Travel and Tours: A wide range of people who are interested in traveling will find inspiration and knowledge from travel guides, itineraries, and advice to complement destination reviews and cultural insights.

7. Eco-friendliness and Sustainability: Content about eco-friendly living, sustainable methods, renewable energy, and zero-waste lifestyles is becoming more popular as environmental awareness rises.

8. Food and Cooking: Meal planning, cooking methods, recipes, and food evaluations satisfy people's enduring interest in gastronomy and the culinary arts.

9. Home Improvement and DIY: Content pertaining to home décor, remodeling, gardening, and crafts might be profitable because of the growing popularity of home renovation shows and the DIY culture.

10. Parenting and Family: Parents and caregivers find resonance in content that addresses child development, family activities, parental problems, and educational options.

11. Learning and Education: Tutorials, online courses, educational information, and learning resources are designed to assist people who want to learn new skills or advance their knowledge.

12. Entertainment and Pop Culture: A large and amused audience is drawn to coverage of movies, TV series, celebrity news, gaming, and pop culture events.

13. Specialized Topics: Niche subjects like pet care, spirituality, gaming, hobbies, or particular vocations may also be lucrative if they have a committed following, depending on your area of expertise and interests.

14. Personal Narratives and Experiences: Readers looking for inspiration and trying to build network may find resonance in memoirs, personal essays, and authentic storytelling on a variety of subjects like conquering obstacles, realizing objectives, or pursuing passions.

15. **Entrepreneurship and Business:** Young small business owners and entrepreneurs find value in insights on beginning a business, entrepreneurship, marketing tactics, and success stories.

In the final analysis, a topic's profitability also hinges on your capacity to produce interesting, high-quality content, comprehend the requirements and preferences of your audience, and successfully monetize your work through channels like affiliate marketing, advertising, sponsored content, product sales, or premium subscriptions.

CONTENT CREATION FORMATS

A key component of effective content marketing is knowing what kinds of content to produce. There are different types of content formats such as articles, podcasts, infographics, videos, blog entries, and interviews.

You may decide to produce different kinds of

content or concentrate on one type at a time, depending on the objectives and purpose of your content strategy.

Here are some of the best forms of material to use in your content development approach. These can be utilized to demonstrate your knowledge and engage prospective customers.

1. Blogs: Among the most popular kinds of material are blog posts. In general, they can easily be shared, readable, and instructive. Make sure your blog posts include attention-grabbing headlines, captivating images, and pertinent keywords.

Writing and posting blog entries is not a difficult task. In reality, artificial intelligence (AI) tools make it easier than ever before to create engaging, high-quality blog entries that are search engine optimized.

Another excellent strategy to spread the word about your message and establish connections with other influential people in your field is to guest blog on other websites.

Among the many advantages of incorporating articles are:

SEO optimization: By include keywords in your writing, you can drive more people to your website.
Engagement: Interesting and educational articles might aid in keeping readers interested.
Authority: Establishing your brand as a recognized authority in your field can be achieved through sharing your knowledge and experience.

The following strategies will assist you in creating quality blog posts:

i. Answer Questions: Think of questions that may be bothering your audience and provide answers.

Gaining the trust of your audience and raising your search engine rankings may both be accomplished by anticipating and providing answers to their questions.

ii. Compare and Contrast Issues and Opinions: If you are an authority in your field, you may assist readers in making informed choices by sharing your professional opinion.

When composing blogs that compare and contrast a method, service, or product, try to be as honest and open as you can. Make a list of every possible advantage and disadvantage that comes to mind. Next, elaborate on how you arrived at those conclusions.

iii. Impart Knowledge: You should consider a few things before using your blog as an instructional tool. When selecting a topic, it's best to start modest. Therefore, pick a particular issue that people in your sector could be curious about rather than discussing a broad topic.

Once you begin to write "how-to blogs", keep the following points in mind:

• Make use of concise phrases and paragraphs with a distinct structure. It will be simpler to follow your directions as a result.
• When explaining new material, utilize examples rather than jargon or technical phrases.
• Keep in mind that you should give basic guidance and easy direction to newcomers; therefore, avoid providing shortcuts or skipping steps.

These pointers assist your visitors in learning while increasing traffic and interest in your instructive content.

iv. Daily, Weekly and Monthly Series: Both you and your readers may benefit from writing a series of entries, which can also help your blog expand. Usually, a series has a predetermined duration. The series can be published every day, every week, or every month on a chosen day.

Content from a series can be readily adapted for different media. For instance, if you have a social media blog, you could create a podcast, ebook, or movie out of a series of blog posts on Instagram Reels.

This approach simplifies the process of thoroughly investigating a certain subject. It helps you become recognized as a thought leader and to create connections and build networks.

v. Quizzes and Surveys: Blog surveys are an excellent method to get input from your audience. This can help with more than just online traffic.

Answers to quizzes and surveys can also help you:

• Identify your audience's preferred content types.

• Determine which goods to promote and sell.

• Grow your social media following.

• Create viral interactive content.

•Prepare for customer service concerns.

Before you begin constructing a quiz or survey, identify your aims. Keeping questions brief and adding incentives can boost response rates.

vi. Curated Content for a Target Audience: Content curation is the process of acquiring information relevant to a specific topic or area of interest, usually with the goal of adding value by choosing, organizing, and maintaining the things in a collection or exhibition.

Content curation will give your most valuable audience members a sense of importance. This could translate to your audience transforming into a network of advocates who promote your content and persuade others to purchase your goods.

Curated content offers you the opportunity to feature statements and analysis from prominent figures in the industry.

2. Podcast and Webinars

Podcasts are online digital audio files that you can download or stream. They give you a unique platform to engage and entertain a larger audience. Listeners can multitask when listening to audio content, such as podcasts while traveling, exercising, or performing other tasks.

You and your brand may be established as thought leaders and industry experts by hosting a podcast. Gaining credibility, fortifying your brand, and winning over your audience are all made possible by sharing insightful information, speaking with authorities, and holding discussions on pertinent subjects.

In addition to textual content, podcasts and webinars are excellent mediums for connecting with audiences. You can record audio versions of your blog entries or expert interviews for podcasts. Through live events and Q&A sessions, webinars are also an excellent approach to engage audiences.

A great podcast would typically start with an excellent idea and then go into further detail using input from experts and listeners. Both educational podcasts and storytelling podcasts are well-liked.

It is important to consider your target audience while producing webinars and podcasts and to modify the material accordingly. To keep listeners interested, employ captivating topics and imagery. In order to assist in promoting your content, you may also think about collaborating with influencers or other brands.

When starting your first podcast, make sure to stick to a regular posting schedule. Additionally, it is a good idea to keep the same framework for each episode.

Furthermore, podcast episodes can be adapted into blog entries, transcriptions, and social media tidbits. This allows you to maximize the impact of

your messaging by distributing your podcast content across a variety of places.
The following tips will help:

i. Thought leadership: The focus of this kind of podcast content is your work history and professional expertise Make sure this content includes case studies and other real-world examples.

Keep in mind that various people are listening to you for different reasons, and they frequently have varying degrees of industry expertise. Provide advise that you believe your audience could use and insights for a variety of listeners.

ii. Interview Influencers: The first step in adding influencer interviews to your podcast is deciding who to interview. Go beyond the most well-known names. Rather, pick engaging visitors who can benefit your audience.

Consider the story you want to tell and the individuals who are most qualified to tell it when selecting guests for your podcast. Make sure to do your homework before you arrive and pose thoughtful and original questions.

Such commitment is evident in the content and increases the likelihood that your visitors would wish to return later or suggest their colleagues for interviews.

Here are some more strategies to make the most of influencer interviews on your podcast:

- Seeking recommendations from your followers
- Encouraging fans of the influencer you've featured to participate

iii. Identify and Discuss Trends: Podcasts can benefit greatly from trending content. This is a clever setting to demonstrate how your products are related to current events, regardless of whether you're talking about a long-term trend or the newest fad.

Although many individuals consume news podcasts on a daily or monthly basis, the majority are timeless, akin to a blog. Years after they were first released, a lot of podcast listeners will still tune in.

This implies that you should connect trends to more significant subjects.

iv. Giveaways and Contests: Contests provide your podcast listeners a rewarding and fun way to get involved and an opportunity for you to increase your subscriber base.

A potential strategy for starting a podcast contest is to share information about a gift or prize on social media. An additional option is interactive contests where listeners can call in to participate in the podcast.

Make sure the award is appropriate and distinctive for your target demographic.

3. Videos: Using videos to educate and engage your audience is a great idea. They can be used to disseminate news about the company, features of new products, or interviews with industry experts.

An additional great way to highlight client success stories and explain how your goods may address their issues is through videos.

Make sure your films have a compelling story, crystal-clear audio, and eye-catching images.

Remember to optimize the titles, tags, and meta descriptions of your videos as well, because this will make them more search engine friendly and raise the ranking of your website.

The following tips will help:

i. Use of Animations: Understanding new or complicated information is made simpler by animation. Hence, utilize animated videos to explain to your audience how your product functions or to highlight a particular issue that it resolves.

Select relatable scenarios that have an obvious connection to your product. Animation, whether in the form of stop-motion or digital animation, can breathe life into a dull subject.

ii. Reuse Content from Blogs: Using the words from your most popular blog as voiceover is another easy video concept. Extended blogs provide excellent material for a series of videos. For your social media posts, you may also condense important blog ideas into brief films. Add your videos to your blog posts after that. This provides another way for readers who stumble into your site through search engines to obtain the information they seek.

iii. Tutorials and How-tos: Video formats are also quite popular for how-to content. If you want to make an effective instructional film, follow simple, straightforward methods. Don't exclude anything, but don't give your audience more than enough information too.

Provide a clear call-to-action at the conclusion and assist your visitors in learning with easy-to-follow visual actions.

Interacting with the comments on these videos is also a smart idea. This could help you think of new video ideas and convince your viewers that you are available if they have any more inquiries.

iv. Product Presentations and Odd Use Cases: Potential buyers may find it simpler to understand how to utilize your products if you provide product demos. You get the opportunity to discuss some of your product design workflows as well.

You can establish a rapport with your audience by discussing the initial problem your product solved and how the solution evolved over time.

They become more trusting of you and your products as a result of this relationship.

Present your product's functionality in an engaging manner. Additionally, you can customize the content of your videos. A fantastic way to introduce specific customers to your items is through video product demos.

4. Image-based Contents: To carry out this sort of content creation, you will typically need the assistance of a graphic designer or a design tool. Infographics, pictures, GIFs, memes, sketches, and screenshots are a few examples of image-based contents.

Make sure you have a solid understanding of the fundamentals when you produce visual content. These include:

• Pick the appropriate subject to convey your point

• Consider composition

• Make use of color and contrast

• Keep it basic and straightforward.

Visual material is great for telling stories quickly. Keep in mind to demonstrate rather than tell as you try your hand at storytelling. To bring out the drama and movement in each scene, try utilizing the environment, attire, lighting, and motion in your photos.

5. Guides, Ebooks and Whitepapers: Whitepapers, guides, and e-books are essential for individuals seeking to establish thought leadership and grow an audience. They are longer-form pieces of material that go over complex topics in-depth and display your knowledge.

These publications involve more effort than other sorts of content creation, but they may be quite effective at captivating readers and increasing conversions.

White papers and ebooks can help your audience learn more about a particular subject. They can also assist them in resolving a pressing issue.

Despite the fact that creating ebooks can be labor-intensive, you can also create ebooks using pre-existing information, such as blogs. The process can be accelerated with an excellent ebook template.

SOCIAL MEDIA POSTS

Social media is an extremely useful tool for your content creation concerns. Approximately 82% of consumers use social media to make shopping decisions. This makes it an ideal location for distributing material and communicating with customers.

Posts on social media include messages, photos, videos, and other types of content that are published on social media platforms such as Facebook, Twitter, and Instagram.

By publishing on social media regularly, you may expand your business's visibility and attract a larger audience by helping to build brand awareness and recognition. You may reach new audiences with your content and brand identity when people interact with and share your posts.

Posts on social media provide you the chance to interact with and get to know your audience. You may build a feeling of community and establish a more personal connection with your followers by answering messages and comments left by people and engaging with them through your postings.

Furthermore, you can post news and updates about your company on social media platforms and ad the link to your website. By doing this, you may increase website traffic and keep your following informed. Social media can also be used to highlight client success stories and demonstrate the beneficial effects that your goods and services have on your clientele.

When writing social media postings, use pictures, hashtags, and short yet informative captions. It is also vital to select relevant keywords so that your content appear in organic search results. Also, use a content format that suits your content creation goal.

Every platform is unique, and not all posts perform the same way across all channels. Still, it's a fantastic way to connect with and expand your audience. Posts on social media therefore, should target particular audiences. For example:

Instagram: Use bright graphics and short words

to tell a story to younger audiences and millennials, who account for more than a quarter of all users.
Facebook: Create compelling material that encourages sharing, comments, and likes.
LinkedIn: Emphasize the professional aspects of your messaging with long-form postings or thought leadership articles.
X (Formerly Twitter): Short tweets with relevant hashtags can help you increase traffic to your website.
It is crucial to keep in mind that social media is a constantly changing platform. To make sure that your postings are interesting and current, you need to keep up with the most recent developments and trends. You can make sure that your content is impactful and resonates with your audience by conducting routine monitoring and analysis.

IDEAS FOR CREATING SOCIAL MEDIA CONTENT
Not every post will perform the same on every social media platform because every platform is a little bit different. Even so, social media remains

a fantastic way to interact with and expand your following.

The following are some ideas that will benefit you as well as aid in the creation of fresh social media content:

1. Talk About Recent Developments in The Industry: Not all of the content your brand shares on social media needs to be original. Sharing news and information about the industry on your page or status has a lot of advantages.

It helps to keep your audience interested and up to date on news and trends. This can be particularly relevant for industries that are decisive, where staying current is important. It can also guarantee that you are consistently interacting with your audience.

Whichever social media network you use; you should adhere to a regular routine that benefits your brand.

2. Generate Educational Content: Creating instructional material allows you to teach your audience something new.

Perhaps there is a common problem your consumers have that a simple "how-to-do" video can solve, or there is a topic relevant to your sector that you can write about in a post.

By providing instructional content, you establish your brand as a valuable resource on which your target audience can count on when seeking new information.

Note that most customers prefer to watch short-form videos when learning about a new service or product, so try dividing your instructional social media content into a series rather than a single long post or video.

3. Collaborate with Other Organisations or Influencers: When you collaborate with another firm or influencer, you gain access to their audience, which can greatly enhance your brand's exposure and lead to new followers.

It can also increase your brand's credibility. For example, if an influencer believes in your product, shoppers will have social proof that it is genuine.

Collaborating with others can result in different and distinct content that you would not be able to create otherwise. Furthermore, working with others might lead to future collaborations, joint ventures, and strategic alliances.

4. Share User-Generated Content: Sharing user-generated material on your social media accounts can give credibility to your company by spotlighting genuine people who like your product or service.

It may also lead to increased social engagement and community development because individuals enjoy seeing themselves and their colleagues covered on a company's page.

5. Follow Trends: Participating in trends on social media may seem futile given how quickly they change. On the other hand, it can be a useful strategy for interacting with your followers and raising your profile if you can act swiftly.

Trending content is often given priority on social media pages, which can make it more likely that people will view and share your content. Engaging with trends additionally demonstrates to potential customers that your business is current and aware of global events.

Overlooking current happenings and producing outdated stuff will only drive your target audience away from your brand.

6. Run Giveaways or Competitions: Giveaways and competitions on social media are excellent ways to market your company. Who doesn't like things that are free, after all?

By prompting your followers to like, comment, or share in order to win, can aid in boosting engagement.

Furthermore, by offering a chance to win something, contests encourage your viewers to provide you with their contact information. In the end, this can provide new leads and help your business to sell more.

7. Give Testimonies: A good testimony can determine whether or not a buyer purchases your product or service. Sharing them on social media can be a powerful way to increase your brand's trust and visibility.

Posting user reviews can help develop trust with potential customers by demonstrating that your product works. By spotlighting genuine people and their stories of benefits the derived from your product or service, you can demonstrate to your audience, rather than telling them, how your brand could help them.

COMMON MISTAKES CONTENT CREATORS MAKE AND HOW TO AVOID THEM

While making mistakes is inevitable on any career path, you should be aware of the errors that can be prevent you from moving forward and earning enough money to become a successful content creator.

Whether you're creating graphics, videos, blog articles, or podcasts, there are several typical errors that you should stay away from since they can harm your brand, reputation and business development.

As a content creator, you should steer clear of these six most frequent blunders:

1. Lack of Audience Knowledge: Understanding your target audience's wants, preferences, and pain spots is one of the first steps in creating content. It will be difficult to draw in, hold on to, and engage readers if you don't know for whom you are writing content.

Create personas that reflect the aims, behaviors, psychographics and demographics of your audience by conducting research on them. This will enable you to better adapt your content to their problems, interests, and solutions.

2. Lacking an Actionable Strategy: Creating content is more than just throwing together haphazard bits of information and hoping for the best. A plan that is in line with your goals, brand identity, and value proposition must be precise and consistent. Posting at the same time every day isn't the only way to be consistent. However, you cannot go for extended periods of time without using the internet. Define your consistency. This could be once a day, once a week or once a month

Content types, formats, and channels; themes, subjects, and keywords; content calendar; content analytics and analysis; and your content purpose, vision, and values should all be part of your plan.

You can plan, implement, and measure your content more successfully and efficiently if you have a strategy in place.

3. Failing to Optimize Your Content: The practice of making your content perform better for search engines and your audience while maintaining its quality and relevance is known as content optimization.

Using best practices for content writing, editing, formatting, design, and SEO are all part of it. The use of concise and readable paragraphs, images, videos, and other multimedia elements to enhance your content; the use of keywords, meta tags, and links to increase the visibility and authority of your content, and the use of calls to action to nudge your audience to take action are some of the essential components of content optimization.

4. Non-Promotion of Your Content: Creating outstanding material is worthless if no one sees it. You must promote your content in order to reach your intended audience and maximize its impact.

You can promote your content in a variety of ways, including posting it on your website, email list, and social media accounts as well as working with other content producers, influencers, and industry professionals. Also, you can promote your content by taking part in niche-related online communities, forums, and groups; and by using paid advertisements like Google ads, Facebook ads or YouTube ads.

5. Failing to Engage with Your Audience: Creating content involves two-way communication. To foster advocacy, loyalty, and trust between you and your audience, you must interact with them.

In order to interact with your audience, you can do the following: ask them questions, solicit their opinions and feedback; answer their messages, reviews, and comments; organize challenges, contests, and campaigns using user-generated content; provide incentives, discounts, and rewards; and foster a feeling of community and belonging among your audience.

6. Failing to Develop from The Mistakes You Made: The process of creating content involves continuous learning. It's imperative that you grow from your errors and advance your abilities.

To improve your content creation, you can figure out your strengths, weaknesses, opportunities, and threats; track and analyze the performance of your content using tools like Google Studio,

Google Analytics, and Google Search Console, and set SMART (specific, measurable, achievable, relevant, and time-bound) goals and action plans. These will help you learn from your mistakes.

CONCLUSION

Conclusively, content creation can be as simple as putting pen to paper or starting to type on a laptop. Nevertheless, it is far more difficult to produce quality content that attracts relevant visitors to your website or page. It takes hours of planning and research to create meaningful content that speaks to the issues and provide answers to the queries that your audience is interested in. After it is released, you must continue to keep an eye on the content to make sure the desired outcomes are being achieved. From inspiration to posting to monitoring and optimization, the content creation cycle is a continuum.

Content creation includes a variety of activities such as maintaining and updating websites, blogging, article writing, photography, videography, online commentary, social media accounts, and editing and distributing digital material.

A completed piece of content is not always a flawless content. In reality, there is always room for improvement in every piece of content. Those are the areas of opportunity and it just takes time for them to surface. Traffic, growth, and brand awareness are all facilitated by content creation, which eventually results in higher revenue and sales.

Seeing your content as a product is the greatest approach to maximize its potential. Consider your website's content or social media post as an exciting event and a massive value proposition that you can offer to your audience, rather than just something you produce on a regular basis.

When it comes to product marketing, we frequently consider the name and the package. Packaging in this context refers to the layout of your work, the page design, and any other images you decide to include. In either case, your content will pop off the page and appear much more valuable if you spend more time and care in how you display it. It will be more professional and more entertaining to read if it is filled with eye-catching fonts and high-quality photos.

Your readers will feel as though they are reading something more engaging, which increases the likelihood that they will return and that they will accept what you have to say. The title will serve as the "name" of your product in this instance. Your article's title should express the intrinsic worth; thereby projecting its unique sell point(USP). This is what makes a product stand out from the competition and guarantees its worth. This is crucial when it comes to writing blog articles since, without anything special to offer readers, you are depriving them of a reason to read it and significantly reducing its potential value.

Make sure your audience understands what the article can do for them and why it is important by encompass this unique selling point in the title. genuinely strike on the emotional button and the value proposition.

Try to appear as enthusiastic about your new blog article or your social media post as you would about a brand-new product while promoting your content. And reiterate that there is no cost associated with this incredible, exquisitely presented information.

Additionally, you are not limited to just promoting your material once and calling it a day. Similar to a product, you can continue to market it for many years to come. Periodically reminding people about an old "evergreen" post is quite acceptable. Similarly, you can work on your postings to make them better, update them, or modify their tone a little. This then offers you unrestricted permission to give them another shout-out and locate a more recent, larger audience for them.

You can therefore see that, content has the power to alter how visitors perceive your website and how your followers see and interact with your social media post. So, you must first change the way you view content to harness its benefits.

You must therefore present yourself in the best possible light. The written content ought to be fascinating, captivating, and artistically displayed. Every blog article need to have the vibe of a project and entice readers to keep reading.

Begin to create the finest content you can right now. Then resolve to continue doing this and to put more of an emphasis on offering fantastic value than on the immediate profit margin

www.ingramcontent.com/pod-product-compliance
Lightning Source LLC
Chambersburg PA
CBHW050239230526
45470CB00005B/2024